NEW HORIZONS

science 5~16

KEY STAGE 2   Y3-4

Life around us

Jacqueline Dineen

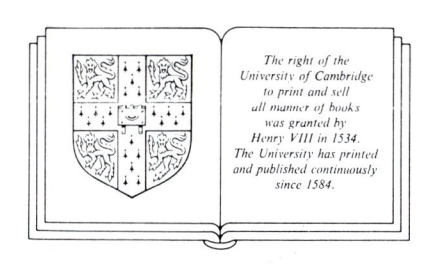

*The right of the
University of Cambridge
to print and sell
all manner of books
was granted by
Henry VIII in 1534.
The University has printed
and published continuously
since 1584.*

Cambridge University Press

Cambridge   New York   Port Chester   Melbourne   Sydney

Published by the Press Syndicate of the University of Cambridge
The Pitt Building, Trumpington Street, Cambridge CB2 1RP
40 West 20th Street, New York, NY 10011-4211, USA
10 Stamford Road, Oakleigh, Melbourne 3166, Australia

© Cambridge University Press 1991

First published 1991

Designed by Pardoe Blacker Publishing Ltd, Shawlands Court, Newchapel Road, Lingfield, Surrey RH7 6BL
Illustrated by Chris Forsey and Dawn Brend
Printed in Great Britain at the University Press, Cambridge

British Library cataloguing-in-publication data
Dineen, Jacqueline
Life around us.
1. Organisms
I. Title II. Series
574

ISBN 0 521 39752 9

Acknowledgements

The author and publishers would like to thank the World Wide Fund for Nature for permission to reproduce the panda logo on page 36.

Photographic credits

t=top b=bottom c=centre l=left r=right

Cover: NHPA

4*t* Karl Switak/NHPA; 4*b* Sinclair Stammers/Science Photo Library; 9*l* Nigel Downer/Planet Earth Pictures; 9*r* Stephen Dalton/NHPA; 10 Heather Angel; 13 Trevor Hill; 15*l* Geoff du Feu/Planet Earth Pictures; 15*r* Dr Jeremy Burgess/Science Photo Library; 16 Trevor Hill; 17 Robert Harding Picture Library; 18 Bruce Coleman; 20 Kim Taylor/Bruce Coleman; 23 J. David George/Planet Earth Pictures; 24 Jen & Des Bartlett/Bruce Coleman; 26*l* Oxford Scientific Films; 26*r* Jonathan Scott/Planet Earth Pictures; 27 Tony Howard/NHPA; 29*l* Adam Hart-Davis/Science Photo Library; 29*r* Anthony Bannister/NHPA; 32 ZEFA; 36 Ken Balcomb/Bruce Coleman; 39 M. I. Garwood/NHPA; 41 Robert Harding Picture Library; 44 Simon Fraser/Science Photo Library; 47*t* Richard Waller/Ardea; 47*b* Sarah Ewington/The Hutchison Library; 49*t*, 49*b* Nigel Cattlin/Holt Studios; 50 Mary Evans Picture Library; 52*t* E. A. Janes/NHPA; 52*b* Joe Blossom/NHPA; 53 Roger Wilmshurst/Bruce Coleman; 55 Stephen Dalton/NHPA; 56 J. B. Blossom/Aquila Photographics; 57 Trevor Hill; 58*l* Heather Angel; 58*r* Trevor Hill; 60 Linda Williams.

NOTICE TO TEACHERS
The contents of this book are in the copyright of Cambridge University Press. Unauthorised copying of any of the pages is not only illegal but also goes against the interests of the author.
For authorised copying please check that your school has a licence (through the Local Education Authority) from the Copyright Licensing Agency which enables you to copy small parts of the text in limited numbers.

Contents

Introduction	4
Suiting the environment	6
All sorts of plants	8
Plants with seeds	10
The life cycle of a flowering plant	12
Finding out about plants	14
Using plants	16
Animals in their groups	18
Life in miniature	20
Life in the water	22
Life in the air	24
What is a mammal?	26
How do animals reproduce?	28
What happens when living things die?	30
How do we know about the past?	32
Finding a home	34
How people affect the environment	36
The seasons	38
Life on the move	40
The start of farming	42
Farming today	44
Farming around the world	46
Farming the land	48
Storing food	50
Farm babies	52
How green is your farmer?	54
Why do people keep animals?	56
Caring for animals	58
Too many pets?	60
Key words	62
Index	64

Introduction

Plants and animals are living things. There are thousands of different plants. Some are big, like the giant trees in the rain forests. Some are tiny.

Think of all the animals on the Earth. There are huge elephants and tiny insects. Some animals live in the sea, others live on the land.

Each type of plant and animal differs from the others in some way. But, all living things grow and in the end they die.

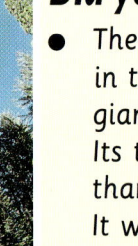

gibbon (South East Asia)

tamandua (South America)

iguana (South America)

Did you know...?

- The biggest plant in the world is the giant sequoia tree. Its trunk is more than 10 m across. It weighs 360 times more than an elephant! These trees are the largest living things on Earth.

- The smallest flowering plant is the duckweed. It is 0.5 mm long and 0.2 mm wide.

Can you find out which are the largest and smallest animals in the world?

Earth's environments

The Earth is different everywhere. It has different **climates**. It is hot in some places and cold in others. In some places it rains a lot. Other places are dry. The Earth also has different types of soils and rocks. It

toucan
(South America)

flying frog
(Borneo)

lowland gorilla
(West Africa)

The rain forests are home to half of all the world's species. There may be 30 million types of insect alone.

has mountains and seas. There are open grassy **plains** and thick forests. The climate and the surroundings form the **environment**. Each type of animal and plant has learned to survive in their own environment.

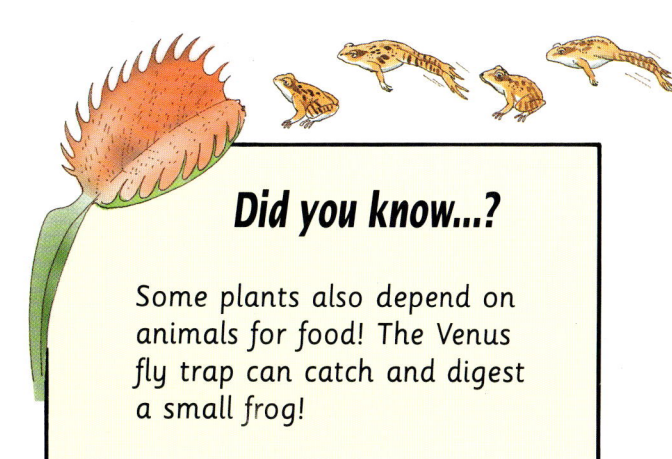

Finding food

All animals depend on plants for food. Some animals eat plants. Other animals are meat-eaters. They hunt and eat the plant-eaters. So, in a way, they are eating plants, too.

The same thing happens in the water. Tiny water animals eat tiny water plants. Small fish eat tiny water animals. Big fish eat small fish. This is called a food chain.

Did you know...?

Some plants also depend on animals for food! The Venus fly trap can catch and digest a small frog!

More about: climates pp6-7   food chains p35   soils pp48-49

Suiting the environment

tundra
Long, severe winters and short summer season. The soil just below the surface is nearly always frozen so plants are mainly mosses and lichens, forming a rough, scrub landscape.

Plants need certain soils and climates to grow. Animals need food, shelter and safety from their enemies. They find a place to live, or **habitat**, which gives them these things. Sometimes plants and animals have to **adapt** or change to suit the environment they live in.

Fish and most other water animals can breathe and live underwater

Food is hard to find in winter, so squirrels store nuts. Hedgehogs go to sleep until spring.

temperate climate
Cooler with four seasons. In winter it is cold. In spring plants start to grow. In summer it is warm and in autumn it starts to get cool again. Plants and animals have adapted to the climate.

The cactus can grow in the desert because it can store water.

tropical climate
Hot with a lot of rain. Plants grow huge. In the tropical rain forests, many animals live in the trees and eat the fruit that grows on them.

Did you know...?
- Camels can live without drinking water for 3 weeks. They drink up to 130 litres of water at a time.
- The gerboa (desert rat) never drinks water. It gets its water from the plants it eats.

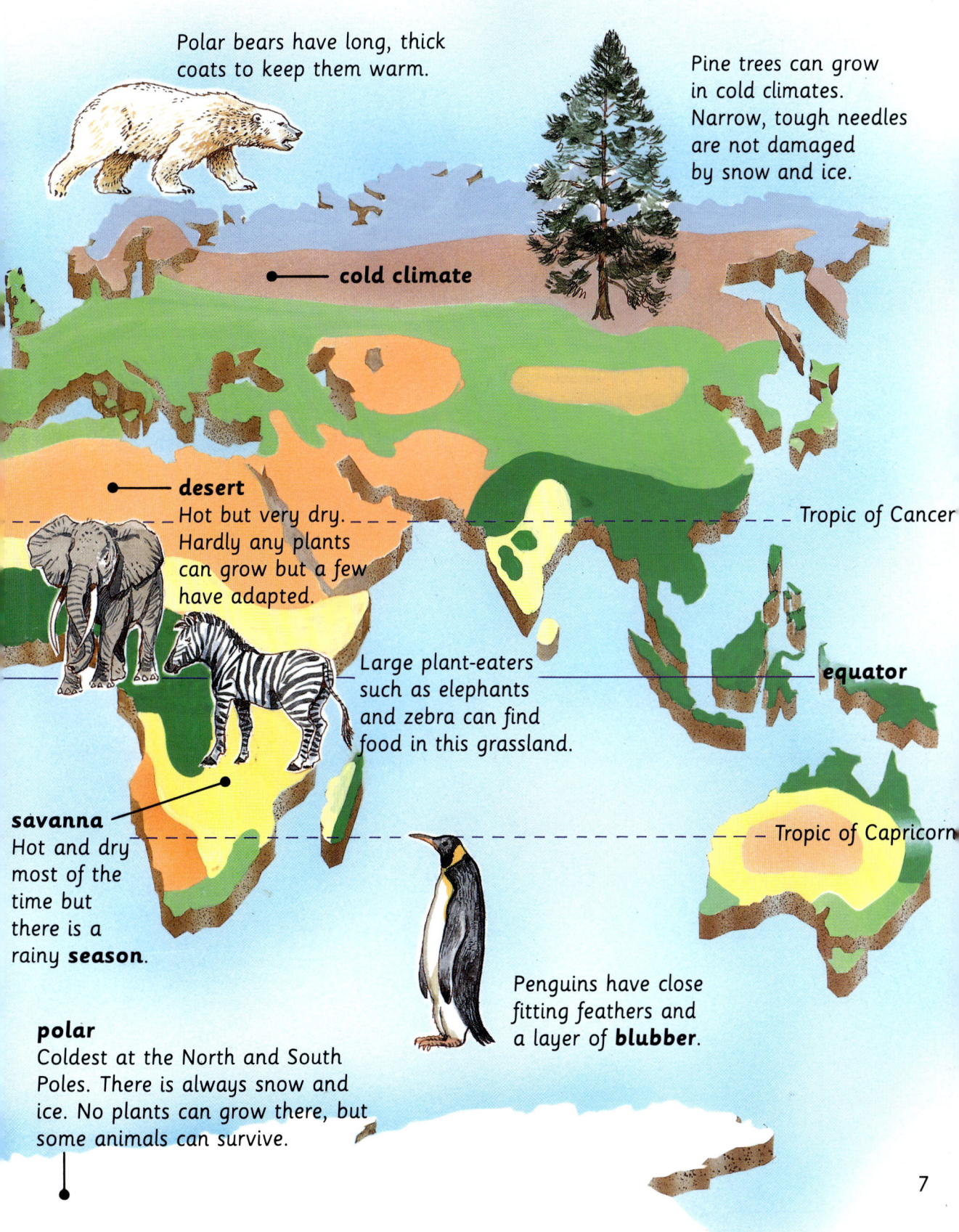

Polar bears have long, thick coats to keep them warm.

Pine trees can grow in cold climates. Narrow, tough needles are not damaged by snow and ice.

cold climate

desert
Hot but very dry. Hardly any plants can grow but a few have adapted.

Tropic of Cancer

Large plant-eaters such as elephants and zebra can find food in this grassland.

equator

Tropic of Capricorn

savanna
Hot and dry most of the time but there is a rainy **season**.

Penguins have close fitting feathers and a layer of **blubber**.

polar
Coldest at the North and South Poles. There is always snow and ice. No plants can grow there, but some animals can survive.

More about: life in the water pp22-23   seasons pp38-39

All sorts of plants

Plants are very different from animals. They cannot move about. Animals stop growing when they are adult but plants can stop and then start growing again.

How a plant makes its own food

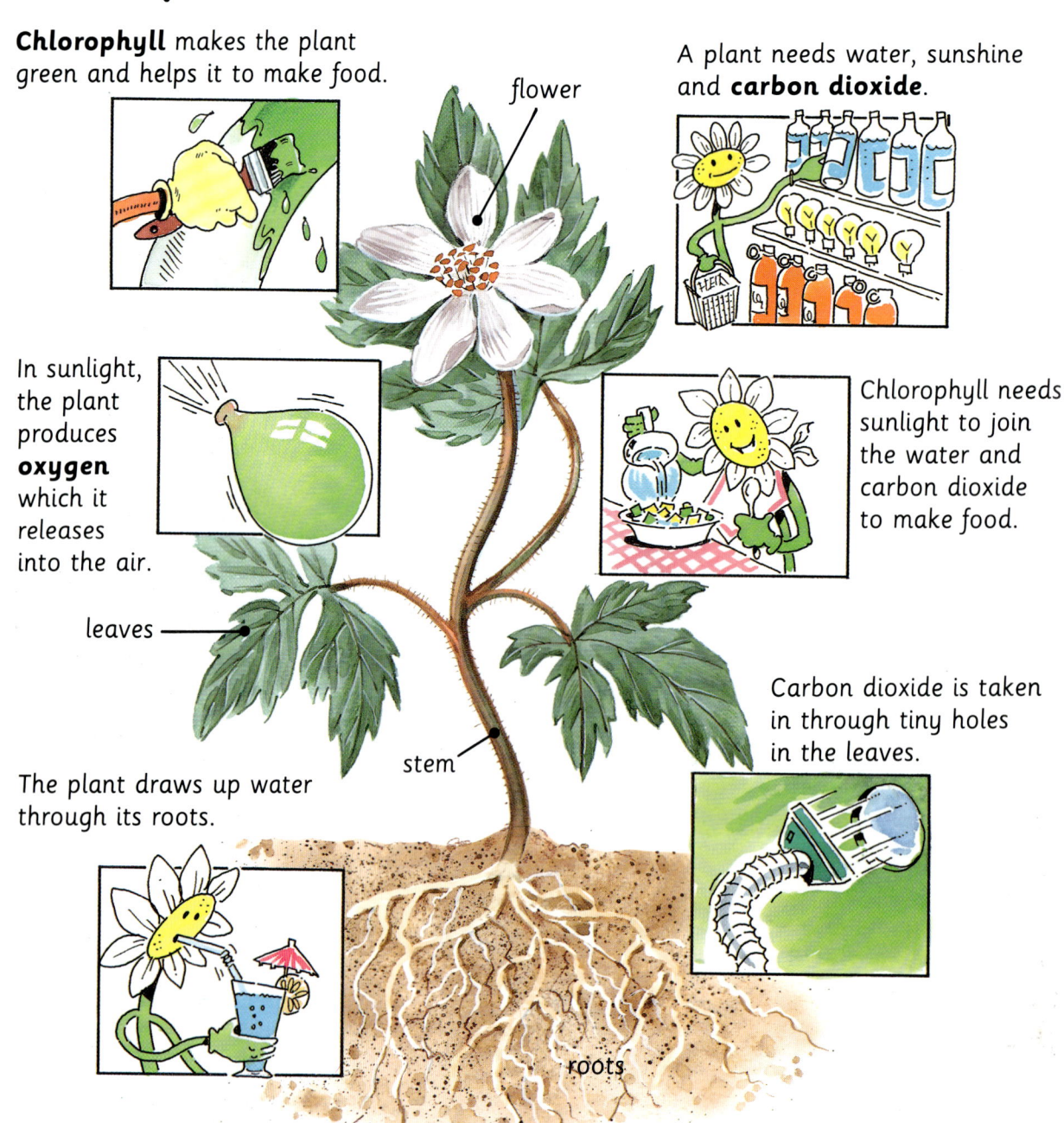

Chlorophyll makes the plant green and helps it to make food.

A plant needs water, sunshine and **carbon dioxide**.

flower

In sunlight, the plant produces **oxygen** which it releases into the air.

Chlorophyll needs sunlight to join the water and carbon dioxide to make food.

leaves

Carbon dioxide is taken in through tiny holes in the leaves.

stem

The plant draws up water through its roots.

roots

Did you know...?
The Amazon rain forests in South America produce one-third of the Earth's oxygen.

Mosses are simple plants. They grow along the ground where it is damp, or on fallen tree-trunks and walls.

The green scum on the surface of ponds is really millions of tiny plants called **algae**. Some algae are so small that you can see them only with a microscope. Seaweeds are types of algae. They do not have roots or flowers like some other plants.

Mushrooms, toadstools and lichens

Mushrooms and toadstools are types of **fungus**. Fungi are a bit like plants but they do not have leaves, stems or roots. They do not contain chlorophyll so they cannot make food. They have to feed on other things. Have you seen fungi growing in tree-trunks? They take their food from the wood. The mould that appears on rotting food is a type of fungus. Lichens are made from fungi and tiny algae. Have you seen yellow lichens on rocks or old buildings?

You can eat some mushrooms but many funghi are poisonous. Some can kill you. It is very dangerous to eat any fungus unless you are sure what it is.

Did you know...?
Ferns have **fronds** and roots but no flowers. In Britain, ferns grow to about 1 m high, but in the tropical rain forests giant tree-ferns grow to 25 m.

More about: flowering plants pp12-13   types of plant pp14, 16-17

Plants with seeds

Most plants have seeds. Seeds are the plant's way of making sure that new plants will grow. If plants could not **reproduce**, or produce new plants, they would soon die out.

Seed plants

Seed plants have roots, a stem and leaves. Most have flowers. Some flowers are big, like roses. Others are so tiny, you can hardly see them.

Types of seed

The fruit of a plant contains its seeds.

Broad bean seed
In each seed is everything that is needed for a plant to grow except oxygen and water.

- hard shell protects the inside from hot or cold weather
- shoot
- roots grow if the soil is right and there is water
- food for the young plant

poppy — hard seed case full of tiny seeds

okra — fruit, seeds

berry — fruit, seeds

tomato — fruit, seeds

Spreading the seeds

When seeds are spread out, they grow into new plants. It is better if they get away from the parent plant. Seeds such as sycamore 'wings' and dandelion 'parachutes' are blown by the wind. Birds and animals eat fruit and berries and drop the seeds. Some seed cases stick to animal fur. Squirrels and other animals hide nuts. Sometimes these take root and grow.

Coconuts float on the sea. Some are swept on to beaches and grow into new palm trees.
Some seed cases 'explode', sending the seeds flying through the air.

Seeds without flowers

Pines, firs and other **conifers** produce seeds but they do not have flowers, they have cones. The seeds form in these cones. Birds eat the seeds. One bird, the crossbill, has a beak with special crossed tips for getting seeds out of cones. Some seeds fall to the ground and grow into new trees. Seeds also pass through birds and come out in their droppings.

Nuts are another type of seed.

horse chestnut — seed case

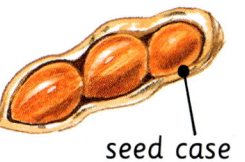

peanut — seed case

In the mid-1950s, some seeds from a plant called the Arctic lupin were found in Canada. They had been frozen in ice for about 10 000 years, but when they were planted some grew into healthy plants!

coconut — seed case

wheat — seed

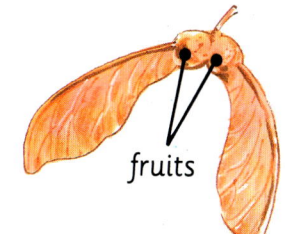

sycamore 'wings' — fruits

dandelion 'parachutes' — fruits

Did you know...?
- Orchids produce the smallest seeds.
- The coconut is the biggest seed.

How many of these seeds have you seen? Can you find more examples of types of fruit, seed case and seed?

More about: conifers p15 flowering plants pp8, 12, 14 seeds p13

The life cycle of a

Before the seed can grow, there must be enough soil for it to put down roots. There also must be water. The seeds cannot grow without water.

All flowers have the same parts. The flower produces seeds to make new plants. It cannot produce seeds unless it has been **pollinated**.

Water softens the seed case so that the seed can sprout.

The seed pushes up a stem. The roots draw water from the soil and anchor the plant in the ground.

Leaves grow and the roots spread under the soil. Big trees like oak would topple over without their large, spreading roots.

Buds appear, covered by **sepals.** They are usually green and look a bit like leaves. Sepals protect the flower developing inside.

When the flower is ready, the sepals part and the flower opens out.

Flowers have male and female parts, just as there are male and female animals. Some plants have male and female parts on the same flower. Others have male and female flowers on the same plant, or on separate plants.

Bulbs, tubers and corms

Daffodils, tulips and some other plants grow from bulbs instead of seeds. Bulbs are food stores. The onion is a bulb you can eat. Bulbs stay in the ground over the cold winter. In spring, the food stored is used to make a new plant.

A potato plant grows from a tuber, which is the part you eat. Crocuses grow from corms. These store food for the plant in the same way as bulbs.

flowering plant

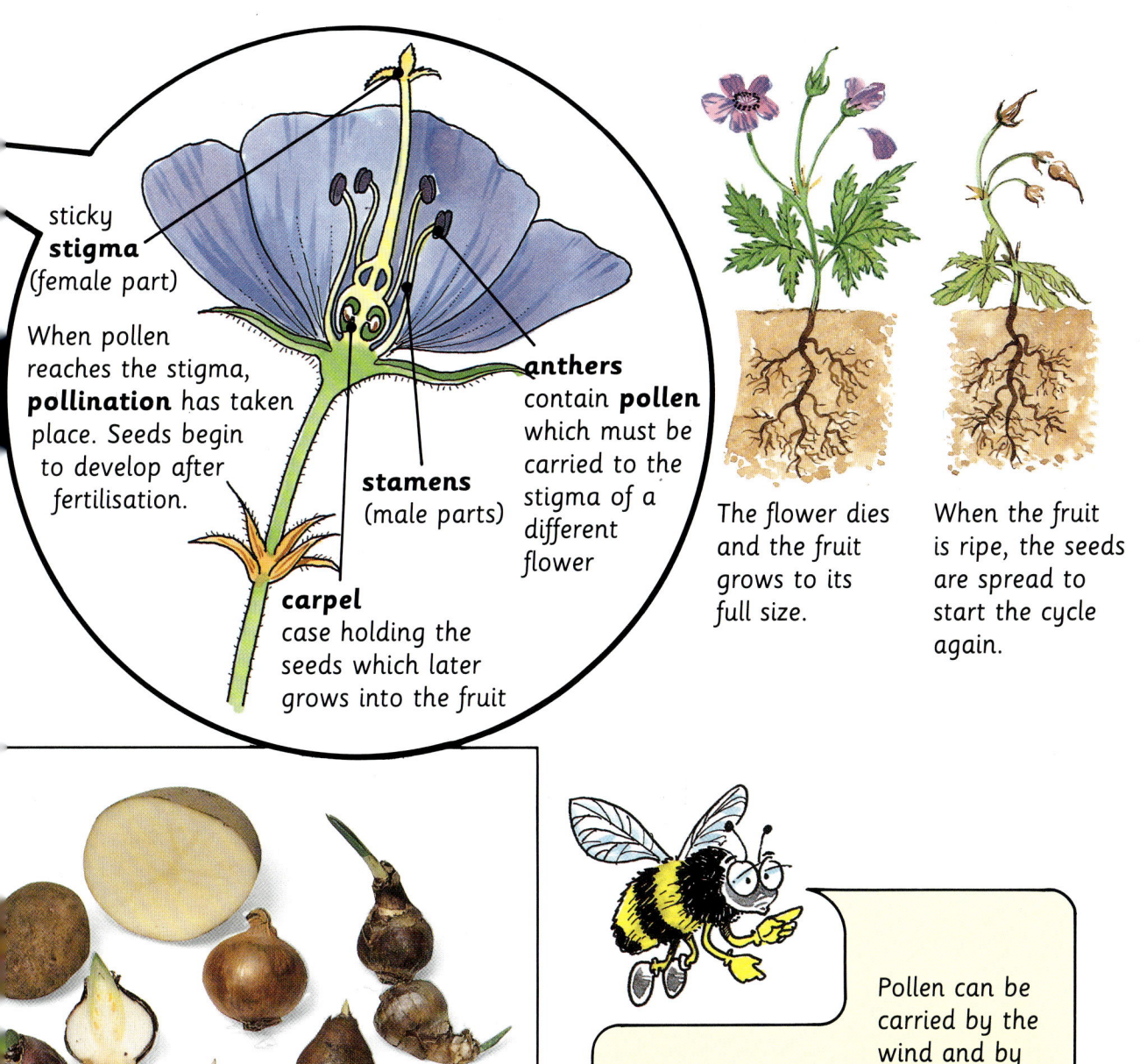

sticky stigma (female part)

When pollen reaches the stigma, **pollination** has taken place. Seeds begin to develop after fertilisation.

anthers contain **pollen** which must be carried to the stigma of a different flower

stamens (male parts)

carpel case holding the seeds which later grows into the fruit

The flower dies and the fruit grows to its full size.

When the fruit is ripe, the seeds are spread to start the cycle again.

Pollen can be carried by the wind and by insects. Bees feed on sugary **nectar** made by the flowers. Flowers which attract insects usually have colourful petals or a sweet smell.

More about: how a tree grows p15   pollination p15   types of flower p14

Finding out about plants

How can you tell which plant is which? There are several ways of **identifying** them. The colour of the flower will give you a clue. You can look closely at the petals and leaves, too.

Flower

four petals
poppy

five petals
dog rose

cluster of petals
clover

bell-shaped flowers
bluebell

orchid

petals of uneven shape
dandelion

single flower head

cow parsley
cluster of flower heads

Leaves

snowdrop

all the way up the stem
white deadnettle

short and narrow

dark green
light green
primrose

watercress

smooth

hairy
lily of the valley

red campion

long and narrow
wild daffodil

rounded
waterlily

heart-shaped
convolvulus

Stem

long
short
violet

foxglove

thick
hogweed

thin
forget-me-not

harebell

single stalk

branches
heather

14

Spreading the pollen

Bees drink nectar from flowers and pollen sticks to their legs and body. When they land on another flower, some of this pollen is left behind.

Some plants have special ways of protecting themselves. Thistles and roses have thorns on their stems. Stinging nettles drive fine hairs into an animal's skin. Some plants and berries are poisonous and have a bitter taste.

Some plants use the wind to spread their pollen. The wind blows pollen from catkins to female flowers.

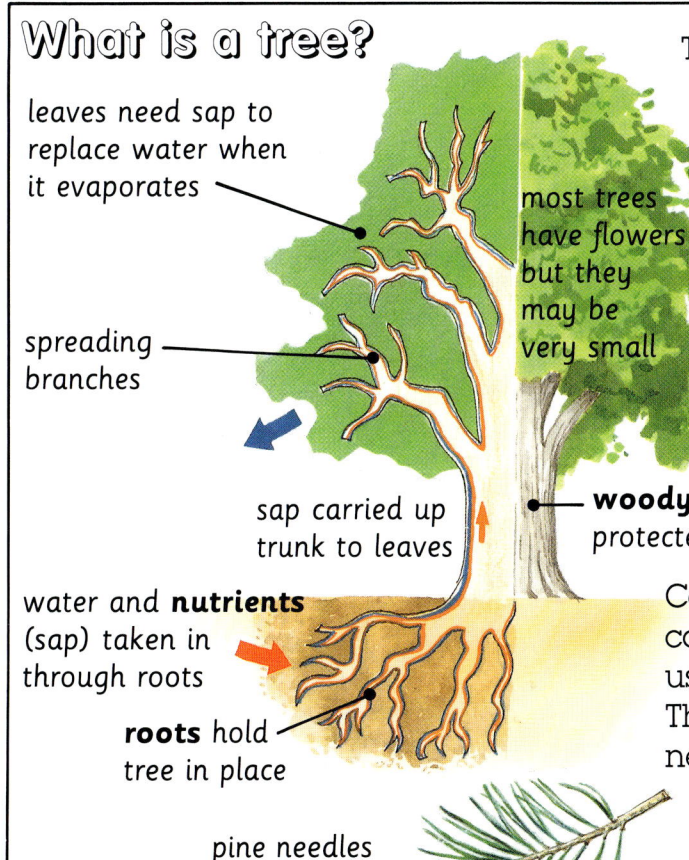

What is a tree?

- leaves need sap to replace water when it evaporates
- spreading branches
- sap carried up trunk to leaves
- water and **nutrients** (sap) taken in through roots
- **roots** hold tree in place
- pine needles
- most trees have flowers but they may be very small
- **woody trunk** protected by bark

Trees such as oak, beech and sycamore are called broad-leaved trees. Their leaves need plenty of sunshine and water to make food. They are sometimes called hardwoods. Their wood is usually hard and takes years to grow.

sycamore leaf

Conifers are sometimes called softwoods. Their wood is usually soft and grows quickly. They have narrow leaves called needles which are tough. They can survive in very cold climates without much water.

More about: broad-leaved trees pp17, 38   conifers p11   pollination p13

Using plants

The first people on Earth were hunters and gatherers. They learned a lot about the plants growing around them. They found grasses, berries and fruit to eat.

Later, people discovered how to burn wood to make fires. They found that some plants, such as cotton and flax, have fibres which can be made into cloth. Others can be made into medicines and **dyes** for cloth and wool.

Look around your house or classroom. How many things are made from wood? We cut down millions of trees to make these things. Wood is used as a fuel. Paper is made from wood chips.

South American Indians found that trees growing wild in the Amazon jungle contain a liquid which can be made into rubber.

About 120 years ago, seeds were taken to Asia. Today, there are huge rubber **plantations** there, especially in Malaysia.

Plants for food

Today, plants are used to make a variety of things. Here are examples of plants we use to make foods.

wheat
corn
vegetables
sugar cane
fruit

Look at this picture. Try to find out which plants are used to make the drinks shown.

Can you think of other plants which are used to make foods?

Cork from the cork tree.

Raffia is a palm tree. Parts of the leaves can be woven into mats and baskets.

We spin and weave cotton into cloth.

Sacking and rope made from the stems of hemp or jute.

Today, plants often have been replaced by **chemicals** and **manufactured** materials in making dyes and cloth. But, in the Amazon rain forest, some people still pick fruit and berries to eat. They use plants for all their medicines and dyes. They make baskets from leaves and stems.

Did you know...?
In Brazil, an area of rain forest the size of a football pitch is cleared every second.

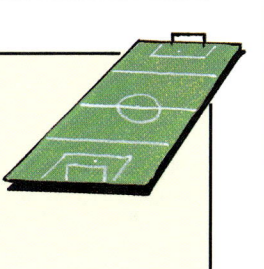

Chopping down forests

Forests of broad-leaved trees such as oak, beech and the tropical mahogany and teak take a long time to grow. When people began to clear land for farming, they chopped down forests.

Trees spread their roots and hold the soil together. When a lot of trees are cut down, the soil can **erode**. That means it is washed away by rain or blown by the wind. This can make the soil poor for growing plants.

The only big forests of broad-leaved trees left today are the tropical rain forests. Now, these are being chopped down, too. This is harming the environment. The rain forests are home to an enormous variety of plants and animals. Their habitats change as the trees are cleared.

More about: broad-leaved trees p15 food plants p43 rain forest p5

Animals in their groups

There are many different types of animals. You are an animal. So is a fly. So is a blackbird or a shark. Animals can be divided into separate groups.

Mammals

Includes cats, dogs, elephants, lions, and tigers. You are a mammal, too. Most mammals give birth to live babies.

Birds

Animals that have feathers and wings. Most can fly. Birds lay eggs.

In which parts of the world do you find the most reptiles? Why is this?

How groups are the same

The different groups have some things in common. Many mammals and birds have claws or **talons** for catching food. Many animals have an outer shell to protect their soft body. Some have colours which warn of danger. Others have markings which match the background so that enemies cannot see them. This is called **camouflage**.

Reptiles

Includes snakes, lizards, turtles and crocodiles. Reptiles cannot control the **temperature** of their bodies. They become cold if the temperature around them is cold, and hot if it is hot. Most reptiles lay eggs, though some snakes and lizards have live babies.

Fish

Animals that live in water and cannot breathe on land. Most fish have fins and a tail to swim with. Fish lay eggs.

All these animals have a backbone. Animals that do not have a backbone include jellyfish, crabs and lobsters, and all the insects.

Amphibians

Includes frogs, toads and newts. They usually lay eggs in water which hatch into tadpoles. As they grow they change so that they can live on land. Many frogs and toads spend most of their adult life on land.

Nocturnal animals

Some animals sleep during the day and come out at night. These are called **nocturnal** animals. Foxes, hedgehogs and most owls are nocturnal animals. They often have big eyes which can see in very dim light. Cats are animals that like to go out at night. Their eyes gleam in the dark.

More about: birds pp24-25 fish pp22-23 mammals pp26-27

Life in miniature

You can study different habitats right on your doorstep. If you look in the garden, in woods, under logs and stones, you will find all sorts of minibeasts.

Slugs and snails can be a nuisance in gardens because they eat young leaves and vegetables. In hot weather, they hide in damp places to stop their body drying out. They come out at night or after rain to feed.

A snail's body is protected by its shell. Thrushes get at the body by smashing the shell against a stone. Snails have shells of different colours. Some match their background, making them hard for birds to see.

Dragonflies skim about over streams and ponds, looking for a place to lay eggs.

wasps

bees

ants

Did you know...?

Snails move very slowly. The slowest snail creeps along at a speed of 2·5 cm a minute!

Grasshoppers and crickets live in long grass. They 'chirp' by rubbing their back legs against their wings.

Spiders **prey** on insects such as flies. Many spin webs to trap their prey. You may have seen spiders' webs inside your house.

Centipedes and millipedes have a lot of legs. Centipedes live under logs and stones and eat small animals. Millipedes live amongst grass and leaves, under logs and sometimes in compost heaps. They eat rotting plants.

earwigs

A woodlouse has a hard shell and seven pairs of legs. Woodlice live in dark, damp places. You may find them under old rotting logs.

Earthworms live in soil and eat rotting plants. A worm has no legs.

All insects have six legs. Spiders have eight legs, so they are not insects.

More about: habitats pp34-35 insects p22-23, 38 snails p56

Life in the water

Small animals live on the banks. Birds such as ducks, coots and moorhens nest among the reeds and rushes.

Some water animals can breathe underwater, others cannot. Ducks, newts, and water voles hold their breath underwater but come to the surface for air.

Many insects lay their eggs in the water where the **larvae** hatch out. Mosquito larvae, dragonfly **nymphs** and others stay in the water until they are fully developed. Then they crawl out and fly away.

A pond is full of tiny insects. Some live on the surface such as pond skaters and whirligig beetles.

Water boatmen lie upside down on the surface and paddle along with strong legs.

Underwater plants and animals need oxygen, just as those on land do. Water plants such as duckweed produce oxygen.

Water beetles and water spiders carry air bubbles around with them so they can stay underwater for a long time.

Pond snails slide along rocks, feeding on plants.

When water plants and small animals die, they sink to the bottom. Worms and midge larvae live on the bottom and feed off this layer.

Life in the water is quite different from life on the land. You can learn about it by studying a pond.

The water scorpion crawls across plants or along the bottom in shallow water. It has a long breathing tube which reaches to the surface of the water.

Pike, carp and trout are freshwater fish. They swim in ponds and in rivers and lakes.

In a rock pool

Rock pools ae left when the tide goes out. If you look in a pool you may see starfish, sea anemones and small jellyfish. Seaweed grows on the rocks. Tiny fish called blennies sometimes hide underneath. You may see tiny crabs scuttling about or a hermit crab peeping out from a shell. The rocks may be covered with barnacles. Mussels and limpets stick to the rocks at low tide. They may be picked off by seagulls looking for a tasty snack.

The fish which live in the sea are saltwater fish. They include cod, plaice, sole, herring and mackerel. Salmon lay their eggs in the river and the young fish swim back to the sea.

More about: birds pp24-25 insects pp20-21

Life in the air

Birds have wings and are covered with feathers. Those that fly have to be light but strong. Their bones are hollow which makes them light. Birds fly by flapping their wings using strong breast muscles. The wings push against the wind and help the bird stay in the air.

Flightless birds

Birds are designed for flight, but some types are too big and heavy. Over millions of years, their wings have become smaller and weaker because they are not used. Ostriches from Africa are heaviest. Penguins, rheas from South America, cassowaries and emus from Australia are also flightless.

How birds are different

Beaks

All birds have beaks to get at their food. You can tell what kind of food a bird eats by the shape of its beak.

Finches have short, strong beaks for cracking seeds open.

Herons and other water birds have long pointed beaks for catching fish.

Birds of prey such as hawks, buzzards and owls catch small animals. Their beaks are hook-shaped to tear their food.

Swallows and swifts have beaks which gape wide to trap insects as they fly along.

Most birds build nests and lay eggs. The parents have to find food to feed the chicks. Some chicks, like ducklings, can feed themselves as soon as they hatch. The mother duck stays with them to protect them from danger.

Birds have a constant body temperature. This means that the temperature of their body stays the same whatever the temperature of the air around them. Their feathers help to keep them warm.

Nests
Birds build many types of nest.

Housemartins and swallows build mud nests under the eaves of houses.

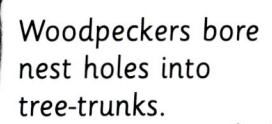

Woodpeckers bore nest holes into tree-trunks.

Tits nest in holes in tree-trunks or in boxes provided by us.

Skylarks nest on the ground in grassland.

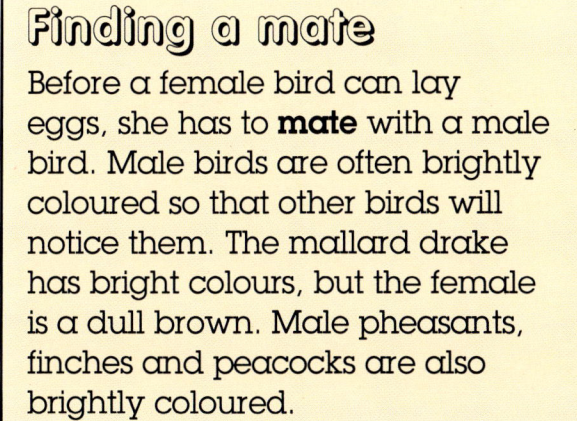

Did you know...?

- Hummingbirds flap their wings at more than 50 beats a second. They are able to hover in front of flowers and suck nectar from inside. They can fly sideways, backwards and even upside-down!
- Albatrosses hardly ever flap their wings. They glide on strong winds over the sea. Their wings stretch 3 m from tip to tip.

Feet

Most birds have claws for gripping the branches of trees.

Birds of prey have strong talons for gripping and tearing food.

Ducks have webbed feet for swimming.

Finding a mate

Before a female bird can lay eggs, she has to **mate** with a male bird. Male birds are often brightly coloured so that other birds will notice them. The mallard drake has bright colours, but the female is a dull brown. Male pheasants, finches and peacocks are also brightly coloured.

Female birds are often duller so that they can hide from enemies while sitting on the eggs.

Sometimes, the male and female parents take it in turns to sit on the nest and keep the eggs warm. These parents often look alike. Birds also sing, fight or perform special dances to attract and protect their mates.

More about: camouflage p18 eggs pp28-29 mating pp26, 52, 61

What is a mammal?

Mammals are warm-blooded animals with hair on their body. All mammals breathe air and have a backbone. In nearly all mammals, the babies develop inside the mother until they are ready to be born.

Mother's milk

Mammals produce milk to feed their young. When the babies are born, they **suckle** or drink milk from their mother. They do this until they are old enough to eat solid food.

How do mammals reproduce?

In most mammals, the baby develops in the mother's **womb**. The baby gets food and oxygen through the **placenta**. A baby develops from an egg inside the mother. Before this can happen, the egg must be **fertilised** by a male. During mating, the male passes millions of **sperms** into the female. The sperms are in a

Life cycle of a rabbit

Rabbits spread quickly because they can **breed** often. The female (doe) mates with a male (buck).

Did you know...?
- The largest mammal is the blue whale. It is about 35 m long and weighs over 130 tonnes.
- The smallest mammal is the pygmy shrew. It is only 6 cm long.
- The lightest mammal is the bumble-bee bat from South East Asia. It weighs less than 2 g.

liquid. They are too tiny to see, except with a microscope. The sperms swim towards the egg. If a sperm joins with the egg, a baby may develop.

Kangaroos are a type of mammal called **marsupials**. Their babies are born before they are fully developed. They crawl into the mother's pouch where they continue to grow.

Mammals behave in different ways. Bats fly through the air, monkeys climb through the trees, kangaroos hop about on strong back legs. Whales, seals and dolphins live in the water like fish, but they cannot breathe underwater. They have to come to the surface for air.
How many other differences can you think of?

Rabbits often have nine babies at a time and they can produce up to eight **litters** in a year.

While she waits for her babies to be born, she builds a nest in the burrow.

When they are born they have no fur. Their eyes are closed. They feed on their mother's milk.

The baby rabbits grow inside her. They will be born a month after mating.

When they are six months old, they can produce babies themselves.

After two weeks, their eyes open. Their fur grows and they are big enough to come out of the burrow. They begin to nibble grass.

More about: eggs pp28-29   mammals p18   reproduction pp52-53

How do animals reproduce?

Animals mate in different ways. Male mammals and birds pass sperms into the female. Female fish, frogs and toads lay eggs and the male releases sperms into the water to fertilise them. Insects lay eggs which hatch into larvae or grubs. Reptiles also lay eggs.

The yolk provides food for the developing chick. The chick starts as a tiny dot in the yolk.

yolk

white

A chick from an egg

Birds may lay several eggs in a nest. They sit on the eggs until they hatch. This is what happens to a hen's egg.

After five days, the chick has a head and backbone.

Some birds hatch without feathers and with their eyes closed. The feathers grow later.

Did you know...?

The ostrich lays the largest egg. An average egg weighs about 1·7 kg. It measures about 20 cm from end to end.

Sea turtles come ashore to lay eggs. They dig holes in the sand and cover their eggs before going back to the sea. When the baby turtles hatch, they have to scamper down to the sea on their own.

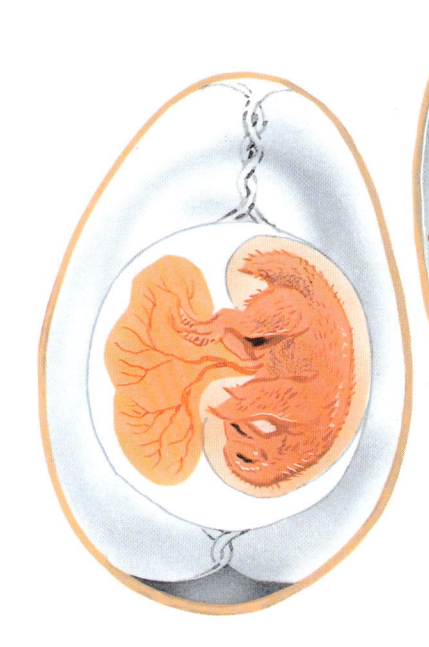

Frogs lay a mass of eggs in a jelly (spawn). Tadpoles hatch from the eggs.

When the chick is fully grown, it fills the shell. It pecks a hole in the blunt end of the egg and struggles out.

After nearly three weeks, a beak, eyes and feet have developed. Its feathers are starting to grow.

The chick has downy feathers and its eyes are open.

More about: eggs p26 reproduction pp52-53 reptiles p19

What happens when

Nothing lives forever. All living things die. So why isn't the Earth covered with dead animals and plants? What happens to them?

Nature has a way of dealing with dead things. Other animals and plants feed on them. Animals and plants which feed on dead things are called **decomposers**.

1 Most broad-leaved trees lose their leaves in winter. The piles of dead leaves are called leaf litter.

On the top are dry leaves. Underneath, it is damp and warm.

2 The decomposers get to work. **Bacteria** and fungi break down leaves and make them rot. This process is called **decay**.

3 Bacteria are all around us, but are too small to see without a microscope.

4 Woodlice, millipedes, slugs and snails burrow through the leaf litter. They feed on the decaying leaves.

5 Earthworms tunnel through the soil. They eat the decaying leaves . . .

6 . . . and mix the soil at the same time. The food from the leaves is taken into the soil. They make the soil richer . . .

. . . so that more plants can grow.

living things die?

7 A tree takes much longer to decompose than leaves do.
Bacteria and fungi feed on the dead wood. Click beetles and stag beetles feed on the wood as it rots. They lay their eggs in the tree and the larvae also feed on the wood.

8 But... when an animal dies, bacteria begin to break down the flesh. The decomposing animal attracts flies such as bluebottles and greenbottles. They lay hundreds of eggs on the animal. The eggs hatch out into larvae called maggots. The maggots feed on the decaying flesh.

Making a compost heap

Gardeners make compost to improve the soil. Compost is the remains of decomposed plants such as grass clippings, weeds and vegetable waste. Wood takes too long to rot.

Layers of plants are piled up and the heap is covered so that heat can build up. Bacteria break down the plants.

Bacteria need damp and warmth to work. The compost heap should be in a sheltered, shady place. It should be built on soil so that earthworms can get into it. The gardener turns the compost over several times while it is rotting. After several months, it is brown and crumbly. It can be dug into the garden.

More about: bacteria p50 earthworms p21 fungi p9

How do we know about the past?

Thousands of millions of years ago there was no life on Earth. Heavy rains fell and formed rivers and seas. There was no oxygen on the Earth because there were no green plants. Even so, tiny living things appeared in the sea.

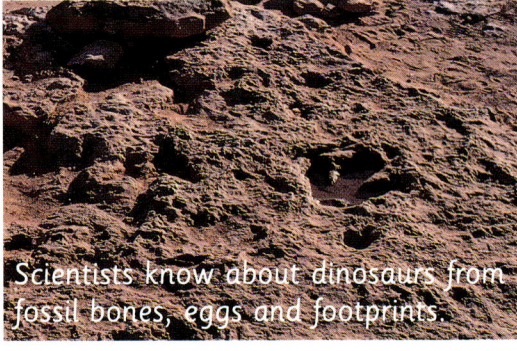

Scientists know about dinosaurs from fossil bones, eggs and footprints.

How fossils are formed

Millions of years ago, when water plants and animals died, they sank into the sand and mud at the bottom.

Rivers wore away rocks and carried more sand and mud into the sea. Thick layers built up.

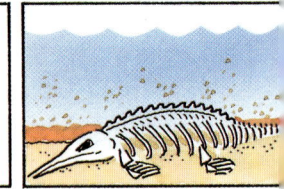

After millions of years, the bottom layers were pressed down so hard that they became rock.

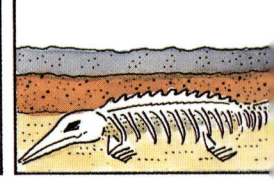

Remains of animals trapped in these layers became **fossils**. Sometimes whole parts are found. Sometimes only prints.

Plants began to grow and produce oxygen. There was enough oxygen for animals to breathe.

The ground was wet and swampy, and covered with thick forests.

500 million years ago

400 million years ago

300 million years ago

Why animals die out

Animals die out if changes on Earth do not suit them. Many amphibians died out because the water dried up. Some managed to adapt to living on dry land. Changes like this can take millions of years to happen.

At the time that most of the dinosaurs died out, the Earth was becoming cooler. Some scientists think that this was caused by something from space. A giant **meteor** collided with the Earth. The dust thrown up would have stopped the sunlight reaching the Earth. If the dinosaurs were used to being warm, they would soon die if they could not adapt.

Did you know...?

Fossils of an ancient fish called a coelacanth have been found. Everyone thought they had died out millions of years ago. Then, in 1938, a fishing boat off South Africa caught a coelacanth. Since then, more coelacanths have been caught.

Animals still die out today. This may happen because they cannot find food or because conditions change. Often, this is the fault of people.

These animals are not drawn to scale. Can you find the real size of the trilobite, the dinosaur and the man?

The weather became hotter and drier. The swamps dried up and most of the amphibians died out.

200 million years ago

1·5 million years ago

60 000 years ago

More about: adaptation pp6-7   endangered species p36

Finding a home

Animals and plants today have all found a habitat that suits them. In Britain, there are woodlands, hedgerows, grasslands, and coastline. They provide food and shelter for many animals. We must protect these habitats if we want the life in them to survive.

Looking at habitats

Woodlands
There are woodlands of broad-leaved trees such as oak and beech. There are also mixed woodlands with conifers. In spring, there may be a carpet of bluebells.

Hedgerows
Hedgerows are made up of smaller trees and shrubs such as hawthorn and elder.

Coastline
Coastline habitats can be tall cliffs, rocks, sand or shingle beaches or flat, muddy marshes.

By the motorway
At the edges of a motorway, there are banks of grassland where people hardly ever go. Seeds from wild flowers grow here. Bees and butterflies feed on the flowers. The grass makes a home for beetles, grasshoppers, spiders, voles, shrews and mice. Yellowhammers, thrushes and linnets nest in the trees and bushes.

Grasslands
Grasslands near rivers and streams have short, tufted, darker green grass. Hay meadows contain long, lighter green grasses and other flowering plants.

Birds of prey, like owls and hawks catch small animals. Smaller birds feed on insects or seeds. Foxes are meat-eaters. They find small animals in the woodlands. Rabbits nibble grass.

More about: conservation p36 habitats pp6-7 rock pools p23

How people affect the environment

People have changed the environment by chopping down forests and hedgerows to make more space.

Some changes such as reservoirs and newly-planted forests do make new homes for plants and animals.

Animals have adapted to live near people, too. Hedgehogs and squirrels live happily in town gardens. Foxes raid dustbins at night. Mice often live in houses. They know they can find food easily near people.

Animals in danger

Animals may die out, or become **extinct**, because people hunt them. The moa and the Tasmanian wolf have died out. The African elephant has been hunted for its tusks and the white rhinoceros for its horn. These animals are nearly extinct.

When there are only a few animals left, it is harder for them to find a mate. The World Wide Fund for Nature is trying to help animals breed and survive. Can you find out more about its work?

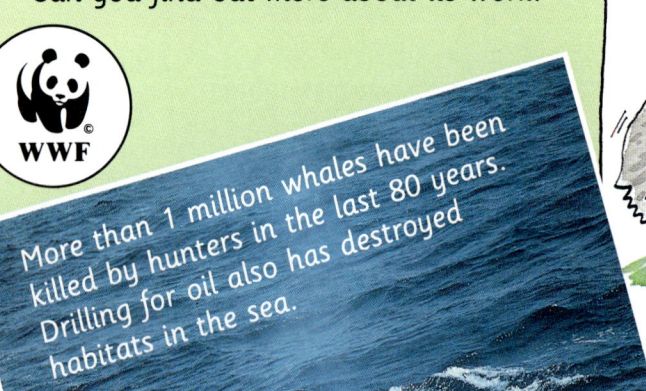

WWF

More than 1 million whales have been killed by hunters in the last 80 years. Drilling for oil also has destroyed habitats in the sea.

What can we do?

We can plant wild flowers for butterflies, provide leaf litter for insects and nesting boxes for birds.

Did you know...?

The dodo was a large flightless bird that lived on Mauritius in the Indian Ocean. About 400 years ago, sailors began to kill the birds for food. The dodo died out.

Dirty water, dirty air

People have **polluted** the air, seas and rivers.

Waste materials and chemicals from factories poison the water and change its temperature.

Oil from ships lies on the surface.

Sunlight cannot shine through dirty water so plants cannot produce oxygen. Nothing can breathe and life in rivers dies.

Fumes and smoke from cars and chimneys pollute the air and kill many plants. They also cause **acid rain**. Poisonous gases from factory chimneys mix with rain and mist. This acid rain kills plants and damages buildings.

Today people try to prevent water pollution. Scientists check the water to see that it is clean.

Food litter attracts flies and rats. Birds and fish are often strangled by the plastic which holds cans of drink together. Small animals like mice and voles squeeze into empty bottles and cans. They become trapped and die of starvation. Swans have been poisoned by lead weights dropped by fishermen or are strangled by their lines.

More about: habitats pp6-7, 34-35   pollution p54   whales p26

The seasons

Winter

Many plants die away. The water plants need is often frozen. Water evaporates quickly from broad leaves so some trees shed their leaves to save water. These are **deciduous** trees.

Evergreen trees such as pine and holly have tough leaves which they do not need to shed.

Birds cannot find insects and seeds to eat. You can help by putting out food for the birds.

Animals cannot find food easily.

Badgers stay longer in their **sets** in the ground and only come out to look for food.

Dormice and hedgehogs **hibernate** or go to sleep for the winter.

Many insects lay eggs and then die. The young insects will hatch out in the spring.

Spring

The weather gets warmer and new buds open on the plants. Blossom appears on trees such as hawthorn and wild cherry. Primroses, daffodils and bluebells are some of the first spring flowers to appear.

Insect larvae appear on plants.

Baby animals are born. They will have several months to grow strong before it is winter again

Hibernating animals wake up and start to look for food.

In the temperate regions there are four seasons. The landscape and the behaviour of some animals changes with each season.

Summer

Many wild flowers are in bloom. You can find foxgloves, buttercups, honeysuckle, dog roses, daisies and many more.

Leaves are fully out from late spring.

Flowers on trees die away and the fruit starts to grow.

Autumn

The leaves on deciduous trees start to turn red and brown. There are berries on the hawthorn, elder and other flowering trees. Rose bushes produce fruits called rosehips.

Animals start to prepare for winter. Some collect stores of food or stop feeding if they are going to hibernate.

On a mountain

A mountainside is like all the seasons rolled into one. It is cold at the top of the mountain. Only dwarf trees grow there. Farther down, the pine trees start to grow. This is called the tree line. The air temperature gets warmer as you go down the mountain. A mixture of pine and deciduous trees grow there. In the valley, deciduous woodlands and meadows need warmer weather.

More about: broad-leaved trees p15 conifers p11 temperate regions p6

Life on the move

Large herds of caribou migrate from the tundra in the Arctic Circle. They spend winter in pine woods in Canada, searching for food.

Some animals **migrate**. This means that they move to another part of the world.

Monarch butterflies live in North America. They spend winter in southern California or Mexico. In spring, thousands fly to the northern United States and Canada.

Brent geese spend the summer in Greenland and migrate to Britain in the winter.

Did you know...?

Some birds fly thousands of kilometres when they migrate. The Arctic tern spends spring and summer in the Arctic. As winter approaches, it flies south to the Antarctic. By the time it has returned to its Arctic home, it has flown more than 40 000 km.

Common eels migrate more than 4800 km to lay their eggs. The larvae grow as they drift back to Europe.

British birds such as swallows, swifts, cuckoos and garden warblers migrate to Africa. Have you seen swallows gathering on telephone wires? They migrate in a huge flock.

People on the move

Some people keep on the move following their herds of animals. They are called **nomads**. The Bakhtiari people are nomads who live in Iran. Every spring, they take their goats, sheep and cattle to new grazing grounds.

The Fulani people keep camels and cattle in the Sahel in Africa. This is a desert area where there is hardly any food. The Fulani have to keep their animals moving to find enough to eat.

People have been following herds in this way for thousands of years. The first farmers were nomads who followed herds of wild animals.

Can you find other examples of routes taken by animals when they migrate?

Near the equator there is a wet season and a dry season. In East Africa, herds of wildebeest spend the wet season in the south. During the dry season, the grass dries up. The herds move north to find new grazing land.

More about:　birds pp24-25　early farmers pp42-43　insects pp20-21

The start of farming

People began to keep animals and grow **crops** about 10 000 years ago.

First, people hunted wild animals for meat and skins. They gathered wild berries, fruit and seeds to eat.

The first crops

The first crops were grown in about 5000 BC. People learned to collect wild grass seeds. They could grow them in one place instead of searching for food. These were the first **cereal** crops.

Domesticated animals

Animals move around in herds to find grazing. The hunters followed them. When they stopped for the night, wolves came to the hunters' fires. The hunters tamed the wolves (dogs). They were the first **domesticated** animals.

People domesticated sheep and goats for wool and milk. Instead of hunting animals, they looked after them, moving around with them to find grazing.

Farmers in China grew rice, barley and millet.

Early farmers settled near rivers where the climate and soil were good. Farmers in the Middle East grew wheat and barley near the Tigris and Euphrates rivers.

Barley was first grown in Britain 5000 years ago. That is about 5000 years after it was first grown in the Middle East! People had to clear dense forests to make fields for crops and animals.

As people found out about crops, they invented tools. The ancient Egyptians invented the plough in about 3500 BC. Ploughs are still used to turn the soil before planting crops.

43

More about: animal farming pp52-53 crops pp46-47

Farming today

Early farmers used simple tools to dig the land. Everything was done by hand. The plough was pulled by oxen or horses. Animals were milked by hand. In Asia and parts of Africa, people still farm small plots of land and use simple tools.

In Europe and North America, farming methods are different today. Machines do most of the work. Farms may be big but the farmer does not need many helpers.

> In Britain, farmers grow cereals such as wheat and barley and vegetables like potatoes, carrots and cabbages.

seed drill

combine harvester

crop sprayer

plough

Machines for crop farming

Before a crop is planted, the farmer turns the soil over with a plough drawn by a tractor. A seed drill is used to sow the seeds. A crop sprayer sprays the growing plants. This keeps them free from pests and disease and adds food to the ground to make the plants grow well. Cereals are harvested with a **combine harvester**. It cuts the cereals, separates the grain from the stalk and cleans the grain. The stalks make straw for animal bedding.

Dairy farming

Cows produce milk for their calves. They store the milk in their **udder**. When the udder is full, the cow has to be milked.

> A person milking a cow has to make it feel like a calf suckling. Milking cows by hand was very slow.

> Today, cows are milked by machine in a dairy parlour. The cows can all be milked at the same time.

> Milking machines have four cups which fit on to the cow's teats.

> They suck the milk out of the cow's udder into a glass jar. From there it goes to a cold storage container. A milk tanker collects the milk from the farm.

More about: animal farming pp52-53   cereal farming pp46-47   milk p50

Farming around the world

Crops need the right amount of sunshine, water and nutrients in the ground.

In countries with a temperate climate, farmers usually sow seeds in spring. The crops grow and ripen during summer. By the end of summer or early in autumn, they are ready to harvest. Crops which grow in Britain and other temperate climates need sunshine and rain, spread throughout the year.

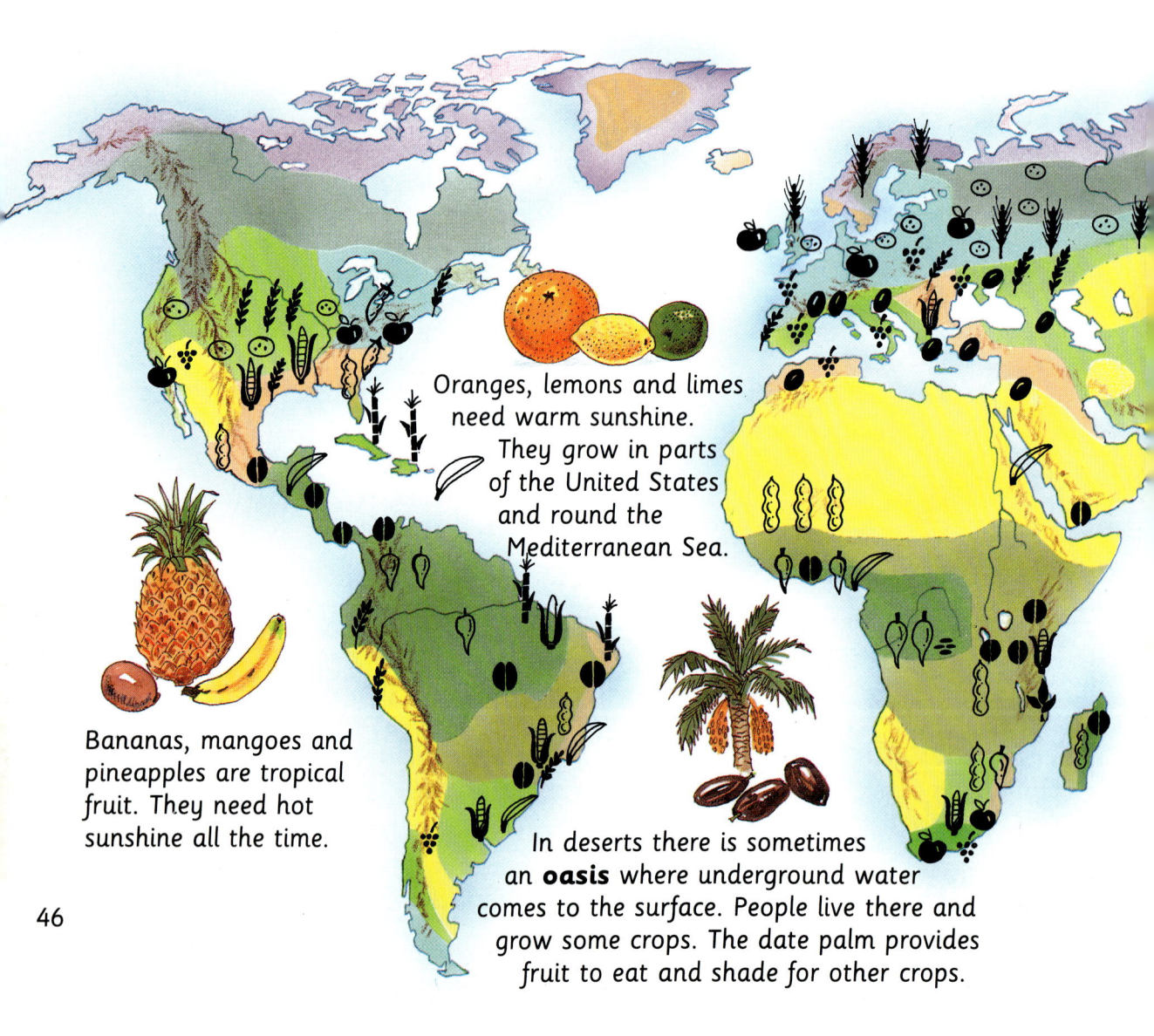

Oranges, lemons and limes need warm sunshine. They grow in parts of the United States and round the Mediterranean Sea.

Bananas, mangoes and pineapples are tropical fruit. They need hot sunshine all the time.

In deserts there is sometimes an **oasis** where underground water comes to the surface. People live there and grow some crops. The date palm provides fruit to eat and shade for other crops.

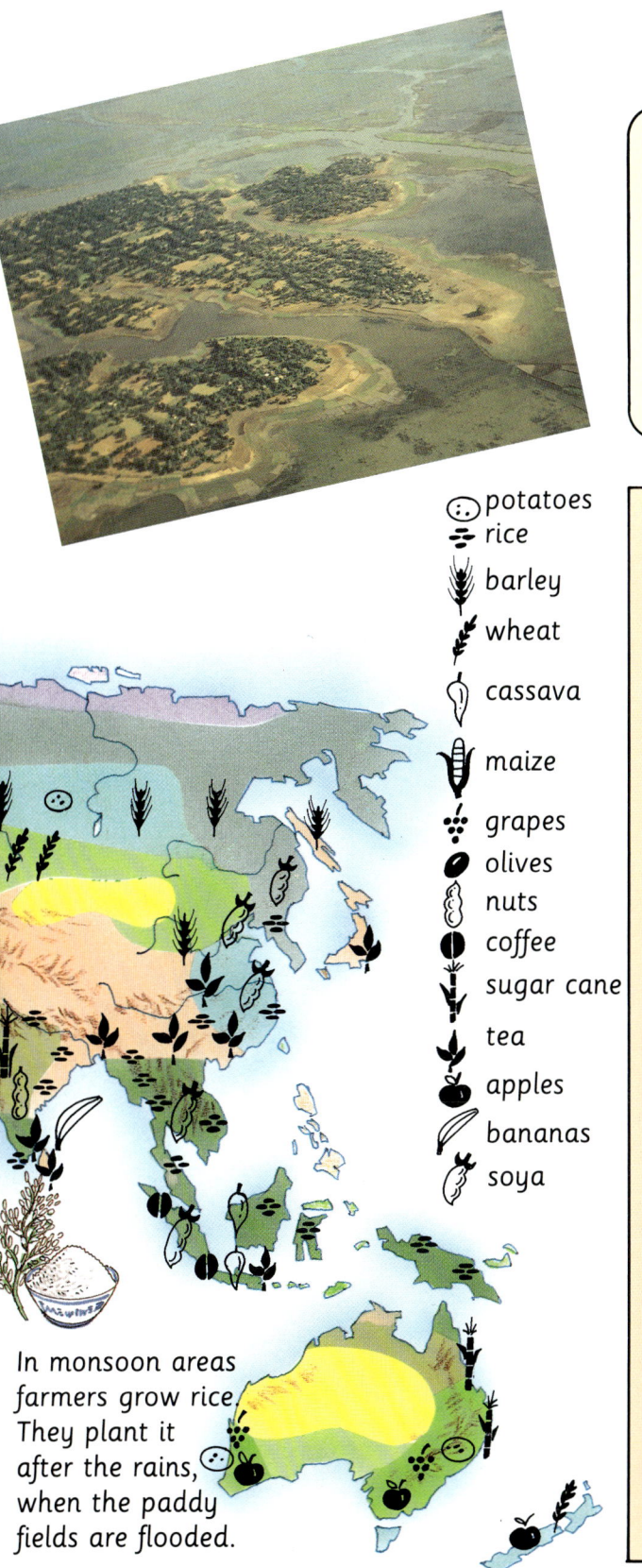

India, Pakistan and South East Asia are **monsoon** areas. Can you find them on the map? Heavy rains fall for days on end in summer. Often, the land is flooded. Many people lose their homes.

potatoes
rice
barley
wheat
cassava
maize
grapes
olives
nuts
coffee
sugar cane
tea
apples
bananas
soya

In monsoon areas farmers grow rice. They plant it after the rains, when the paddy fields are flooded.

Drought

The African grasslands are drier than the monsoon areas. Farmers grow a few crops to feed their families. Sometimes the rains are late and the crops die. Ethiopia is in north-east Africa. In 1982, 1984 and 1987, the rains did not come. There was a **drought**. The crops failed and there was a **famine**. Many people died of starvation.

More about: climates pp6-7   crops pp42-45   fruit p57

Farming the land

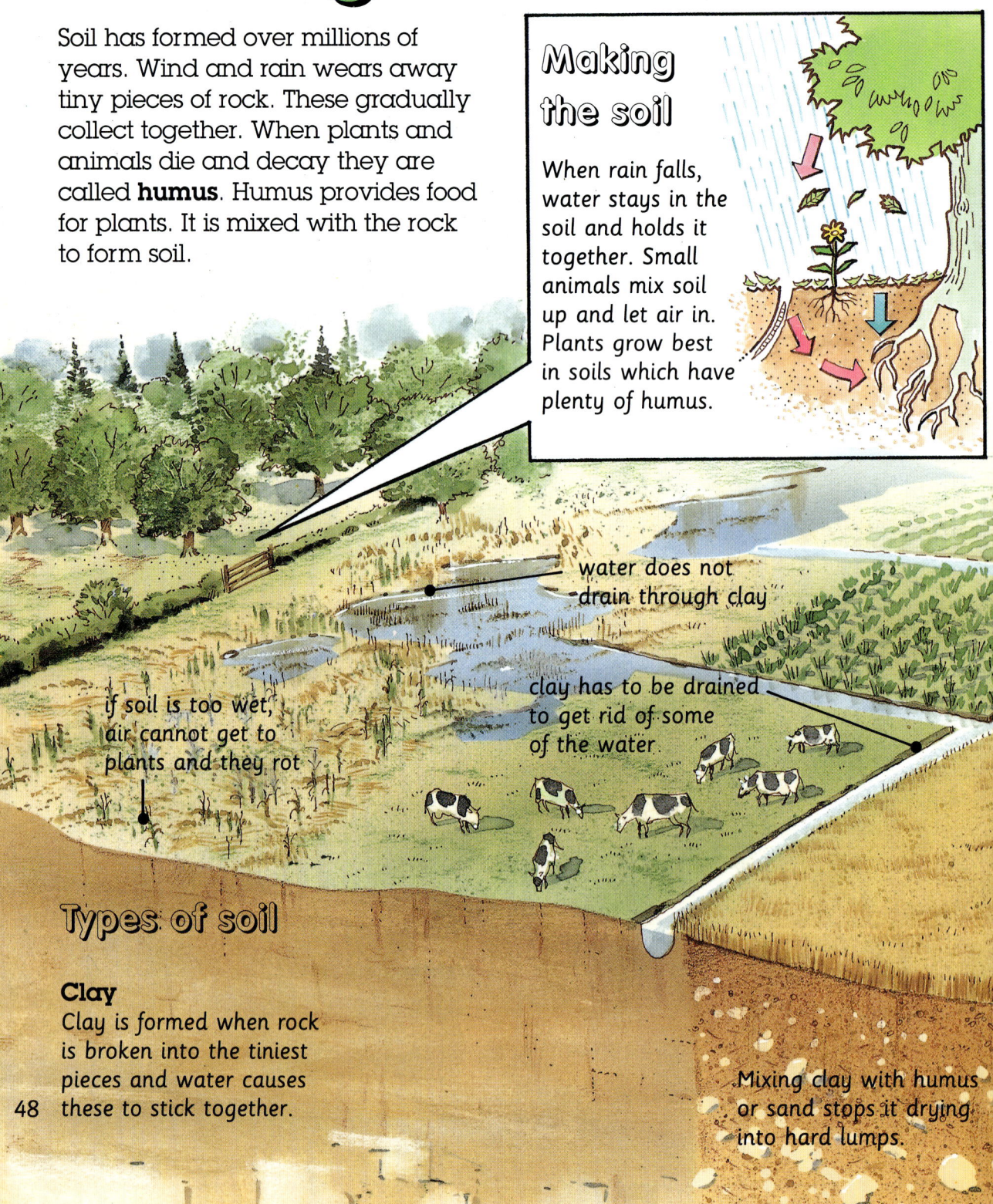

Soil has formed over millions of years. Wind and rain wears away tiny pieces of rock. These gradually collect together. When plants and animals die and decay they are called **humus**. Humus provides food for plants. It is mixed with the rock to form soil.

Making the soil

When rain falls, water stays in the soil and holds it together. Small animals mix soil up and let air in. Plants grow best in soils which have plenty of humus.

water does not drain through clay

clay has to be drained to get rid of some of the water

if soil is too wet, air cannot get to plants and they rot

Types of soil

Clay
Clay is formed when rock is broken into the tiniest pieces and water causes these to stick together.

Mixing clay with humus or sand stops it drying into hard lumps.

Feeding the soil

Farmers can improve poor soil with **fertilisers**. These do the work of the humus. If the farmer has already grown crops in a field, there is not much food left in the soil for new plants. Farmers add fertiliser to this soil before sowing new seed.

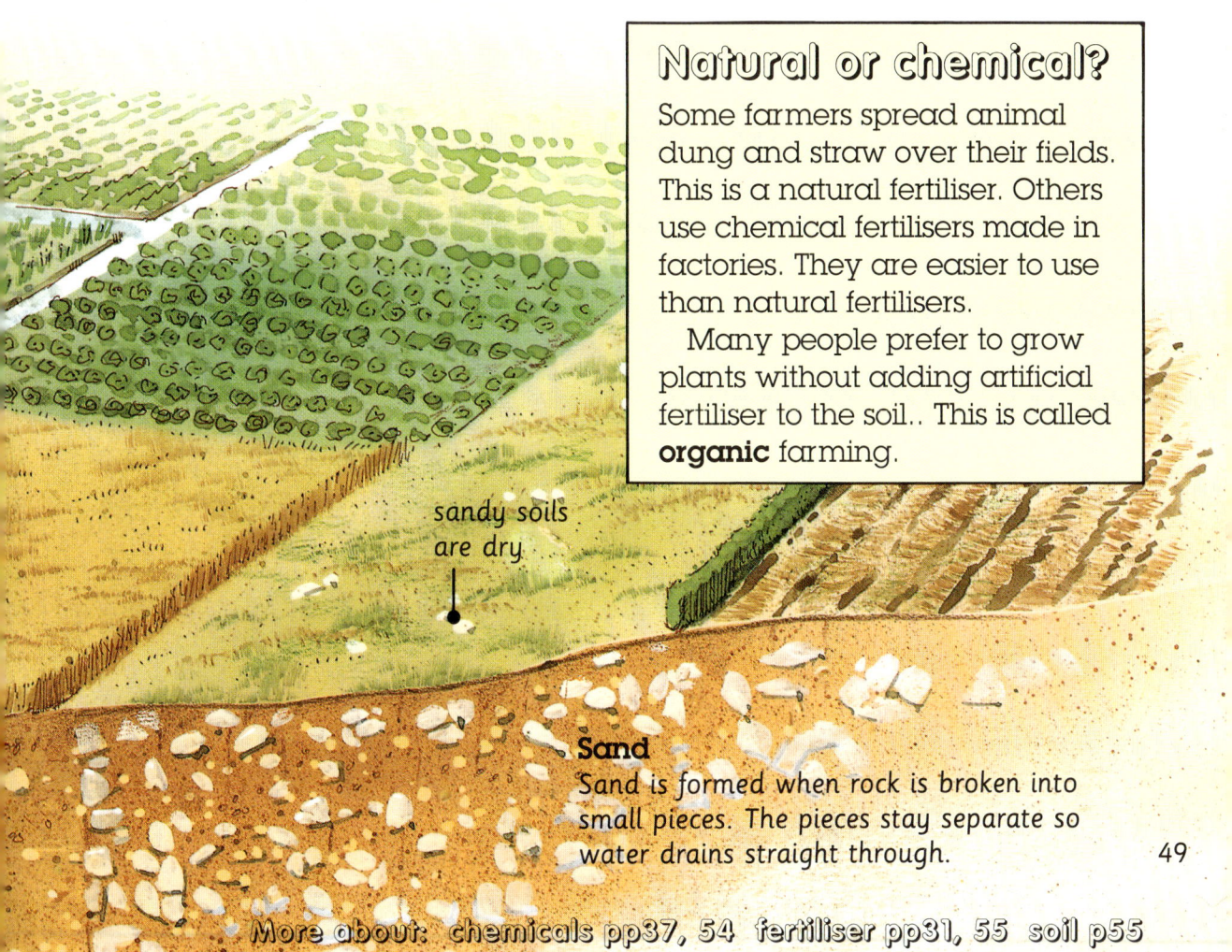

These pictures show the same crop before (top) and after a special fertiliser has been used.

Natural or chemical?

Some farmers spread animal dung and straw over their fields. This is a natural fertiliser. Others use chemical fertilisers made in factories. They are easier to use than natural fertilisers.

Many people prefer to grow plants without adding artificial fertiliser to the soil.. This is called **organic** farming.

sandy soils are dry

Sand
Sand is formed when rock is broken into small pieces. The pieces stay separate so water drains straight through.

More about: chemicals pp37, 54 fertiliser pp31, 55 soil p55

Storing food

In temperate climates, plants do not grow well in winter. People need the same amount of food all year round, so some food has to be stored. Most crops are ready to harvest in summer or autumn.

Fresh food begins to decay if it is kept too long. Food that is going bad contains bacteria that cause food poisoning.
 Salmonella is one type of bacterium found in rotting food. People with *Salmonella* poisoning are very ill for several days.

Preventing decay

Food must be stored carefully to prevent decay. Many bacteria die or stop growing in extreme cold or heat.

One way to store food is to freeze it.

Some foods are sealed inside tins, then heated to destroy any bacteria in the tin. No more bacteria can get in so the food lasts longer.

If all the water is dried out of food, bacteria cannot grow. Dried food keeps for years. Raisins are dried grapes.

Keeping milk fresh

Bacteria can turn milk sour so it has to be treated to kill them. One treatment is called **pasteurisation** after Louis Pasteur who developed it. The milk is heated to a temperature of at least 72°C. It is then cooled quickly and sealed. Pasteurised milk keeps for about four days in a refrigerator.

Can you think of other ways of storing food? How many of these foods do you have at home?

Food from abroad

We can buy fruit and vegetables all the year round from countries where they are grown.

Bananas are picked when they are still green.

They travel to Britain and other countries in refrigerated ships.

When they arrive, they are kept in refrigerated rooms so they do not go bad.

They are ripened in the countries which buy them.

Storing food for farm animals

There is not much grass for farm animals in winter. Cows are fed with **silage** made in a clamp. A clamp is a small walled area where grass is piled up. It is covered with black plastic sheeting to keep out the light. The sheeting is weighted down with old tyres to keep air out. Bacteria begin to work on the grass but do not make it poisonous. They turn it into a kind of pickled grass which will not rot and is good food for animals. Farmers also dry grass to make hay.

More about: bacteria pp30-31 milk p45 temperate climates p6

Farm babies

Many years ago, most British farmers grew crops and kept cows, sheep pigs and **poultry**. Now, many farmers choose just one kind of farming.

Many farmers use most of their land for growing crops. Others keep only one type of animal. There are dairy farms, pig farms and chicken farms. These farms concentrate on producing as much milk, pork and bacon or as many eggs as they can.

Cows and calves

Cows only produce milk to feed their calves. As soon as a calf is **weaned**, the farmer can milk the cow. This is the milk we drink.

The farmer teaches the calf to drink a milky mixture from a bucket. As the calf grows, the farmer gives it solid food to eat. When it is old enough, it is put out in the field to eat grass.

The cow produces milk until the calf is 10 months old. The calf only feeds from its mother for the first few days of its life. Then it is weaned.

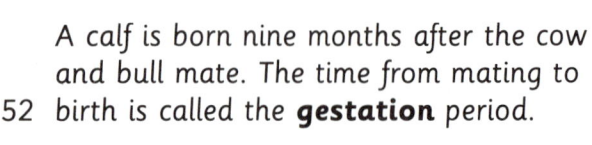

A calf is born nine months after the cow and bull mate. The time from mating to birth is called the **gestation** period.

Lambing time

Most lambs are born in early spring. They grow during spring and summer when the grass is best. The ewe is mated with a ram in autumn. The gestation period is 147 days. Sheep often have twin lambs. The lambs suckle from their mothers. When they are about four weeks old, they begin to nibble some grass.

The life cycle of a pig

Pigs are kept for meat such as pork, ham and bacon. Large pig farms do not have sties.

Chickens and chicks

Hens lay eggs for most of the year but chicks only grow in them if the hen has been mated with a cockerel.

Chicken farmers keep a few hens, called broody hens, specially for breeding young chicks. They lay a clutch of eggs and sit on them to keep them warm until the chicks hatch out. The other hens are never mated. They lay eggs only for sale.

The females (sows) and piglets are kept in fields with huts for shelter. Some are kept in special breeding houses. A sow is old enough to have piglets when she is one year old. She is mated with a male (boar). She can have up to 20 piglets in a litter. Some sows can have two litters in a year.

Piglets suckle from their mothers until they are six or eight weeks old. Then the farmer gives them mixtures of cereals and other foods.

More about: chickens pp28-29   cows p45   milk p45, 50

How green is your farmer?

Before modern machinery, planting and harvesting had to be done by hand, so fields were small. Today, farmers prefer bigger fields.

Early farmers cleared woodland to make farmlands. This destroyed the habitats of many animals and plants. Some, such as the wild boar, died out.

When hedgerows are removed, wild flowers cannot spread their seeds and they die out. Barn owls hunt small animals such as mice and voles which live in hedgerows. The barn owl was once a common bird. Now it is quite rare.

Harmful chemicals

Many farmers use chemical sprays to keep pests away from crops. Small animals such as mice eat the grain and swallow some of the chemicals. As the barn owl catches and eats these, chemicals build up in its body and slowly poison it. Chemical sprays can harm us, too.

When the combine harvester has cut the cereals, it leaves short stalks or stubble behind. If stubble is ploughed into the land, it rots and improves the soil. Some farmers burn the stubble, though. Burning stubble is dangerous as fires can get out of control. It also pollutes the air.

If a farmer grows the same crop in a field every year, the soil loses its goodness. Many farmers **rotate** the crops like this.

Field	Year 1	2	3
A	cereal	root	no crop
B	no crop	cereal	root
C	root	no crop	cereal

cereal (e.g. wheat) → root (e.g. potatoes) → no crop

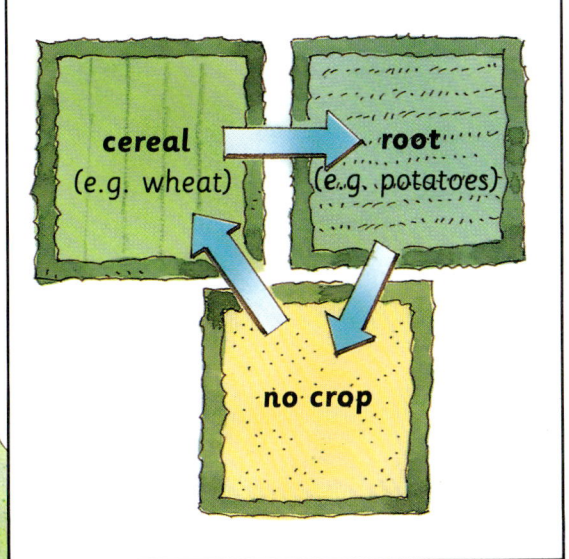

Organic farming

Some farmers grow food the organic way. This means that they use only natural fertilisers. They do not spray their crops to keep pests away.

55

More about: chemicals pp37, 49 organic farming p49

Why do people keep animals?

Most farm animals are kept to provide food. Many people keep animals as pets. Animals are also kept for entertainment.

You can keep animals to study their habits. You can watch birds and small mammals in the garden or the park, or on a country walk. You can see how a snail behaves by making a home for it like this.

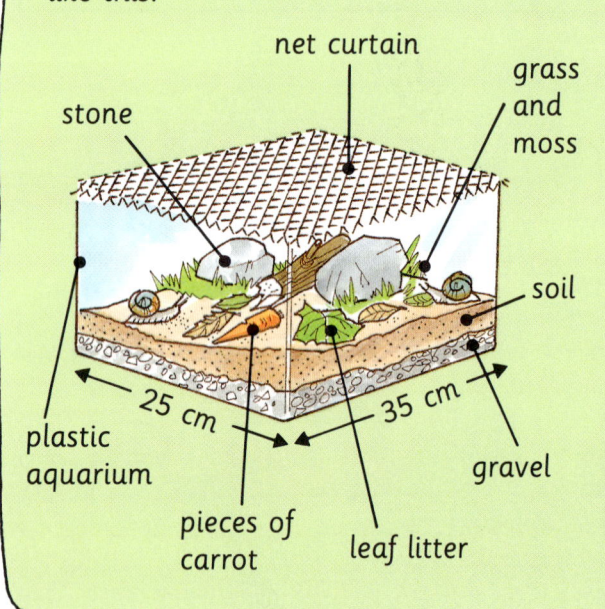

- net curtain
- stone
- grass and moss
- soil
- gravel
- leaf litter
- pieces of carrot
- plastic aquarium
- 25 cm
- 35 cm

The Hawaiian goose was almost extinct. Zoos have been able to breed these geese, and have even returned some to the wild.

Zoos

Animals used to be kept in zoos to entertain visitors. Now, zoos try to save animals which are in danger of dying out. They are safe from hunters. If the zoo has a pair of animals, they might breed. People can see how they behave.

Keeping animals as pets

People keep pets because they love animals. Many people who live alone often keep a cat or a dog for company. Some prefer smaller pets. Rabbits, guinea pigs, gerbils, hamsters and goldfish are popular pets for children.

It's a dog's life

Dogs were first kept to guard farm animals and property. Some were trained to hunt or to round up other animals. Later, dogs were specially bred to carry out different types of work. We still have these breeds today.

> How many breeds of dog can you name? What work do they do?

Did you know...?
In some parts of the world ostriches have been trained to round-up sheep.

Cats in history
Cats were kept in Ancient Egypt 5000 years ago. We know this because they are shown on wall paintings. They guarded food stores and killed rats, mice and snakes. The first pet cats were small wild cats. People think the Egyptians tamed the African wild cat and the jungle cat, which still live in the wild today.

More about: cats pp58, 61 snails pp20, 56 working animals pp42, 52

Caring for animals

Animals need care and comfort. They also need to feel at home.

Large zoo animals like lions and tigers are used to having the savanna or jungle to roam in. They get cramped and bored in a small cage. Today, many zoos keep animals in large fenced-off areas with more room to move about.

Some pets need a lot of care and attention. Make sure you understand all about them before you decide to keep them.

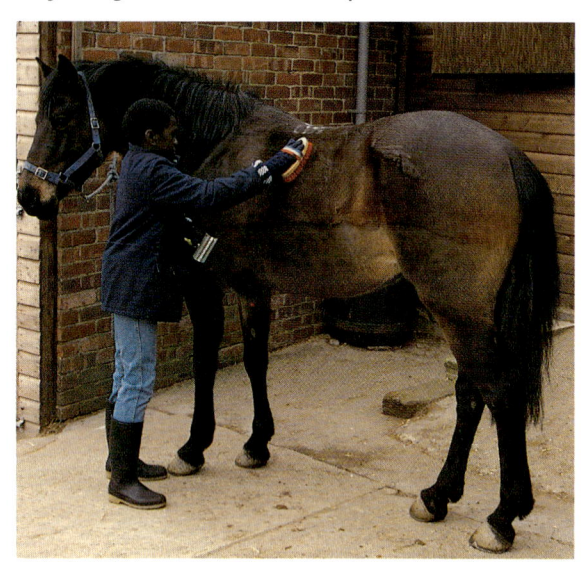

Cats and dogs

Cats and dogs need shelter, food and exercise. Their coats have to be groomed to keep them in good condition. They can be left to wander about in the house and garden. Dogs must be taken for a walk every day, though.

Cats and dogs both like human company. They like to be stroked and patted and made a fuss of. They should not be left locked up in a house all day.

Do not let your dog get on to farmland where it might chase sheep. A dog should always be under control. Big dogs can frighten people, especially small children, so do not let your dog rush up to them.

bored!

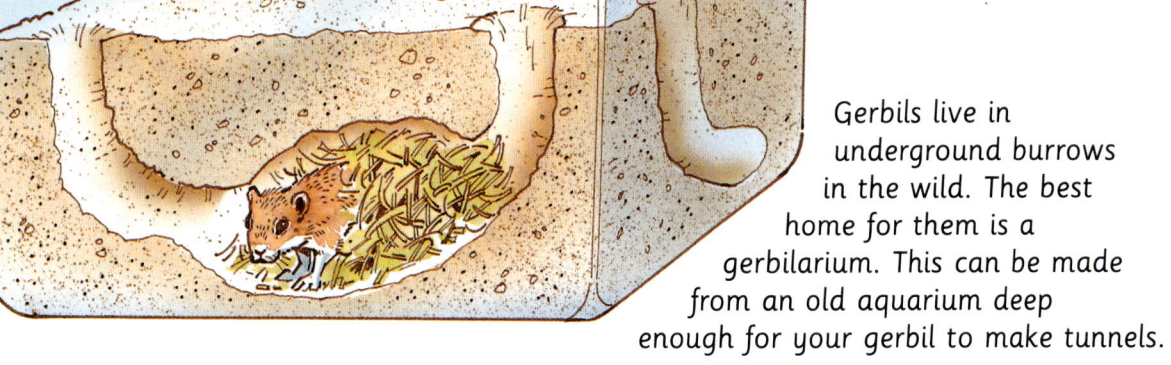

Gerbils live in underground burrows in the wild. The best home for them is a gerbilarium. This can be made from an old aquarium deep enough for your gerbil to make tunnels.

Home, sweet home

Hamsters are nocturnal. They sleep curled up in a nest during the day. They should have an interesting cage. You should not try to wake them up during the day.

Small pets like rabbits, gerbils, hamsters and guinea pigs are kept in hutches or cages most of the time to stop them escaping. You must give them exercise, though, to stop them getting bored. Handle and play with them so they will not be lonely.

Rabbits and guinea pigs can be kept in a wire run during the day. They can run about and nibble the grass. They need shelter in case they are cold. Their hutch should be cleaned out each day and fresh food and water put in.

More about: dogs pp42, 57, 61 pets p60-61 zoos p58

Too many pets?

People like to choose what type of pet they will have, so animals are bred for sale. Many different breeds have been produced.

Owners should look after their pets, but that does not always happen. Sometimes, people buy an animal and then get bored with it.

If dogs and cats are not cared for, they may become strays. These animals may breed and the packs of strays get bigger and bigger.

A visit to the vet

Animals become ill sometimes and have to be taken to the vet.

My puppy needs injections to protect her from disease. Some diseases can kill, so she must have protection.

He has been fighting and his wounds have to be treated.

Controlling the numbers

People can help to control animal numbers. Animals are ready to mate at certain times. When a female dog is 'in season' or 'on heat' she can be kept on a lead or indoors to stop her mating.

Cats are more difficult. They roam about and are likely to mate often. Females can produce litter after litter of kittens. Your cat can be treated by a vet so that it cannot produce young. This is called neutering for a male (tom) and spaying for a female. It is best to get this done when a kitten is five or six months old.

If your dog or cat does breed, you have to find good homes for all the young. This can be difficult. Most people try to prevent this happening unless they are breeding animals for sale.

Will you trim his claws now, please?

I know you feel sorry for your pet. But bringing him to me is the kindest thing to do. We can make sure he stays healthy and happy!

More about: breeding p52-53, 56 pet care pp58-59 reproduction pp28-29

Key words

The meanings of words can depend on how and when they are used. You may find that as you learn more about science the meanings change slightly.

acid rain rainwater which contains harmful gases that can kill plants

adapt to change to suit different surroundings

algae plants which make their own food but do not have seeds

anthers the parts of a flower which contain the pollen

bacteria very tiny living things which are all around us. Some cause disease

blubber a layer of fat which keeps an animal such as a whale warm

breed to produce babies. People can arrange for animals to breed by putting a male and a female together at the right time. A breed of animal is a special type such as a labrador dog or a Siamese cat

camouflage colouring or markings which help animals hide against their background

carbon dioxide one of the gases in air

carpel the part of a flower which holds the seeds

cereal a grass plant which produces seeds that can be eaten such as barley

chemical a substance which acts with another to from a new substance

chlorophyll the substance which makes leaves green

climate the usual weather conditions of an area or country

combine harvester a machine which cuts cereals and separates out the grain

conifer a tree such as a pine or a fir, which has needles instead of leaves and carries its seeds in cones

crops plants grown for food or other uses

decay to rot

deciduous this describes a tree which loses its leaves every winter

decomposer animals and plants which feed on dead things and help them to decompose or rot away

domesticated this describes a wild animal which has been tamed

drought a long dry period

dye a substance for colouring things

environment surroundings

equator the imaginary line around the middle of the Earth

erode to wear away by water or wind

evergreen this describes a tree which does not lose its leaves in winter

extinct an animal or plant that has died out

famine a time when there is hardly any food, often because crops fail

fertilise to join an egg with a sperm so that a baby grows

fertiliser a substance such as animal manure which is put on soil to make plants grow better

fossil a print or the remains of an ancient animal or plant, found in rock

frond the leaf of a fern or seaweed

fungus a plant such as mushrooms, toadstools, or mould

gestation the time between an egg being fertilised and a baby being born

habitat the place where a plant or animal usually lives

hibernate to go to sleep for the winter

humus decayed animals and plants which are part of soil

identify to recognise what something is

larva the young of insects such as flies and butterflies. Larvae do not look anything like the adult insect and they do not grow wings

litter a family of young animals born at one time

manufactured made in a factory

marsupial a mammal which carries its developing baby in a pouch

mate when a male and female mate, they get together to produce young

meteor a small piece of rock travelling through space

migrate move to a warmer part of the world for the winter

monsoon strong wind bringing heavy rain to South East Asia in summer

nectar sugary substance found in plants

nocturnal nocturnal animals are awake at night and sleep in the daytime

nomad someone who moves home often to find food or grazing for animals

nutrients substances which provide food for a living thing

nymph the young of insects such as dragonflies. Nymphs may look a bit like the adult insect

oasis a place in the desert where water comes to the surface and plants grow

organic from plants and animals. Organic farming uses only natural substances instead of chemicals

oxygen one of the gases in the air

pasteurisation a method of treating milk so that it stays fresh for longer. It was discovered by Louis Pasteur

placenta organ in mother's womb which allows food and oxygen to reach the baby and harmful waste to be taken away

plains large areas of flat land

plantation a large area of land where one type of plant or crop is grown

pollen tiny yellow or orange grains produced by anthers

pollinate to move pollen from the male flower or part of a flower to a female flower or part of a flower

pollute to spoil or make dirty

poultry birds such as hens kept on a farm

prey to hunt an animal for food. The hunted animal is also called 'prey'

reproduce produce young

rotate move round

savanna grassy plains in tropical or near-tropical parts of the world

season one of the main periods in a year. In temperate climates, there are four seasons, spring, summer, autumn and winter. In tropical areas, there is a rainy season and a dry season

sepals the outer covering of a flower bud which splits as the bud opens

set badger's home underground

silage food for cattle made from grass which will not rot

sperms reproduction cells which are produced in the body of a male animal

stamens thin stalks in the centre of a male flower, or the male part of a flower

stigma the female part of a flower

suckle to suck milk from the mother

talon strong, curved claw

temperate describes a climate which has warm summers and cool winters

temperature the amount of heat in something, measured with a thermometer

tropical the climate near the equator

tundra cold, treeless landscape near the Arctic. Trees cannot grow there because winters are too cold and dark

udder baglike part of a cow or other milk-producing animal where milk is stored

wean to teach a baby or baby animal to take other foods instead of suckling

womb the special part inside a female where the baby grows

Index

acid rain 37
adaptation 6–7, 36
algae 9
amphibians 19, 22
animal breeds 57

bacteria 30–1, 50
bananas 51
bees 13, 15
birds 18, 20, 22, 24–5, 34–5, 38, 40–41
breeding 57, 61
broad-leaved trees 15, 34
bulbs 12

camouflage 18
cats 57, 58, 60–1
cereals 42–3
chickens 28–9, 53
clay 48
climate 4, 6–7, 38–9, 46–7
cloth 16–17
coastal habitats 23, 35
compost 21, 31
conifers 11, 15, 34
conservation 34, 36
corms 12
cows 45, 52
crops 42–7, 54–5
crop rotation 55
crop spraying 44, 54

dairy farming 45
decay 30–1, 50
deciduous trees 38–9
decomposers 30–1
dinosaurs 32–3
dogs 57, 58, 60–1
domestication 42, 57
drought 47
dyes 16
environment 5, 6–7, 34–5, 36–7
evergreen trees 38
extinction 33, 36; 54

farmers 42–3
farming 42–55
farm animals 42, 45, 51, 52–3
farm machines 44–5
ferns 9
fertilisers 49
fish 19, 23, 32–3
flightless birds 24
floods 47
flowering plants 8–15, 34–5
food chains 5
food plants 16
food poisoning 50
forests 17
fossils 32–3
fruit 46–7, 51
fungus 9, 30, 31

gerbils 59
gestation 52–3
grasslands 35
guinea pigs 59

habitats 6–7, 17, 20–1, 22–3, 32–9, 54
hamsters 59
harvesting 44, 54
hedgerows 34
hibernation 38–9
humus 48–9

insects 19, 20–1, 22–3, 30, 31, 34–5, 38–9

lichens 9

mammals 18, 22, 26–7, 32–5, 38–9
medicines 16, 17
migration 40–1
milk 45, 50, 52
minibeasts 20–1
monsoons 47
mosses 9
mould 9
mountain habitats 39
mushrooms 9

nests 25
nocturnal animals 19
nomads 41

organic farming 49, 55

pasteurisation 50
pets 56–61
pigs 53
plants 4–17, 30–3
ploughing 43, 44, 54
pollination 12–13, 15
pollution 37
pond life 22–3

rabbits 26–7, 59
rain forests 4–5, 9, 16, 17
reproduction 10–13, 25, 26, 28–9, 52–3
roots 8, 10, 12, 15
rubber 16

Salmonella 50
sand 49
seasons 6–7, 38–41, 46–7
seeds 10–13
sheep 52–3
shellfish 23, 35
silage 51
slugs 20
snails 20, 56
soil 48–9
sowing 44
spiders 21
stubble 54

temperature 19, 24
toadstools 9
trees 15
tubers 12

vets 60–1

water life 22–3
wood 16
  hardwood trees 15
  softwood trees 15

zoos 56, 58